Stumbling into Joy is a hymn to the vitality of the human soul and the beauty, depth, and complexity of our lived experience here on earth. This book burns with sacred fire.

— THOMAS YEOMANS, Therapist, poet, painter, and author of *Holy Fire: The Process of Soul Awakening*

Sean Leclaire is a wonderful and unique poet. When you read his work, it is thrilling and dangerous. The text has a truth and relevance that enters the heart of even the most cynical reader. But please try reading him aloud! It gets better as you breathe and speak Sean's words. You encounter the physical power of his words and rhythm. Sound and sense, body and mind, heart and spirit. You feel his fearlessness and his compassion. The title is accurate. You stumble into joy.

— PATSY RODENBURG, Educator, voice teacher, and author of *The Second Circle: How to Use Positive Energy for Success in Every Situation*

Having worked with Sean building high-performance teams for over a decade, I know the authentic, raw, and often shocking power of his life, stories, and poems. The book gives the reader pause for reflection, as well as inspiring one to think of how much more there still is to be and do in life!

— ALAN MAIN, Life science executive and board member of the African Leadership Foundation

There is a space, a stillness that no scientist can find, the mystic's mind. *Stumbling into Joy* is Sean's gift to himself, his son, and us. These poems, potshots, and stories free the mind and open the heart. His fierce spirit awakens.

— MICHAEL CARROLL, Astrophysicist and philosopher

George Orwell insisted we needed to recognize and name the authentic, the genuine, and the true when he said, "In a time of deceit, telling the truth is a revolutionary act." In *Stumbling into Joy*, Sean, then, is a revolutionary actor. He takes a brave, unflinching look at his own foibles and foolishness, as clearly as anyone is ever able to do, without ever looking away. His stories are intimate. Using his natural gift as a radically honest, playful, self-deprecating storyteller, he regales us with descriptions of life learning to be a father, often at the hands or the expense of his delightfully patient son. He reveals through some trial—and a great deal more error—his endless limitations, follies, and human imperfections. All of them familiar, readily shared by us all. Why is this important? Because we have lost our way, and many of us feel bereft of anything at all like shared human joy. His journey is an immersion into deep joy.

— REV. WAYNE MULLER, *New York Times* bestselling author of *Sabbath: A Life of Being, Having and Doing Enough*

Stumbling into Joy is a deep insight into an inspirational life-journey woven together with radical honesty, beautiful language, and authenticity. Sean's unique way of creating beauty with words will touch many souls and can lead to wisdom and transformation. The book is a courageous gift of bringing to the world what is needed right now.

— CHRISTA SCHOENING, Painter and co-founder of The Global Coaching Group

With *Stumbling into Joy,* Leclaire inspires a journey and a respite. Insightful and "inciteful" provoking laughter-out-loud and deep contemplation, especially in his "potshots" so truthful they jab at your ego, if you listen wisely. In the rhythmic midst of this book is an achingly vivid love story of a son-father, whose son fathers his stumble into joy.

—LISA DALTON KERMAN, National Michael Chekhov Association, President, Author of *Falling for the Stars: A Stunt Gal's Tattle Tales*

I'm always floored by the way Sean Leclaire articulates the world as he sees it as an artist and consciousness teacher, but none so much as now with *Stumbling into Joy.* This collection of poems and stories is at times sad but always beautiful, a haunting hymn to the love and struggles we hold for the complex world we all live in. This book is about the multi-faceted experience of living life, where the beautiful and brutal intermingle and are, perhaps, impossible to separate.

—RICHARD RAYMOND, Filmmaker

This book will make you think deeply, but more importantly it will make you feel, to remember your past and your future all in one essay or poem. Occasionally, I had to stop and take a breath. I turned a page and moments later was stunned by the brilliance of less than forty words.

—FRED MILLER, Yoga teacher and author of *How To Calm Down, Even If You're Absolutely, Totally Nuts*

Wonderful, profoundly moving stories and poems that both pull me into a world and illuminate my own. Sean takes us with him on his journey into love. We try, we fail, grace visits us, and we try again. Life shocks us with a slap, then coaxes us with a caress. A freight train thunders by, and no one hears our screams. At length, silence. The sky clears. Stars come out, then tears of joy.

—JAY VOGT, Consultant and author of *Recharge Your Team: The Grounded Visioning Approach*

Reading Sean's work is to come to things that really matter in oneself, to listen inside, to pause from distractions, to meet what counts. Each piece functions as a thought haiku that opens reflection and is demanding in its apparent simplicity. Sean questions how we find joy, affirming that it lies at the center of life, despite all the forces we exercise against it. This is timely subject matter, and Sean's words continue to haunt long after reading.

—ELIOT SHRIMPTON, Artist

T. Dr. Katherine,

Blessings of good
health & joy.

Sean

STUMBLING INTO JOY

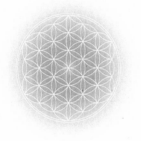

Also by Sean Casey Leclaire

PROSE
Hug an Angry Man and You Will See He is Crying
Mud-Wrestling with my Mind

PLAYS
Men
Small Town Boys
LEELA

STUMBLING INTO JOY

Sean Casey Leclaire

Satya Media
New York

Satya Media, New York 10036

This is a work of creative nonfiction.

For more information, contact Satya Media,
560 West 43rd Street, Suite 20, New York, NY 10036
www.seanleclaire.com

First edition published 2021
Printed in the United States of America

10 9 8 7 6 5 4 3 2 1

ISBN: 978-0-9724859-2-0 (Paperback)
ISBN: 978-0-9724859-3-7 (e-book)

Library of Congress Control Number: 2021903113

⊗ This paper meets the requirements of
ANSI/NISO Z39.48-1992 (Permanence of Paper).

For Beau

There are no shortcuts to sacred places.

Eternity

He who binds to himself a joy
Does the winged life destroy;
But he who kisses the joy as it flies
Lives in eternity's sun rise.

—WILLIAM BLAKE

Table of Contents

NOTE TO THE READER

Where does joy live?

Somewhat of a mystery, but there are clues.

Our minds create pleasure and its kissing cousin pain but not joy.

When we breathe, there's a natural pause at the top and bottom
of the breath.

A four-part rhythm:

In, pause, out, pause … breathe.

Joy lives in the pause.

An empty mind is full of joy.

The silencing of thought tends to coax joy to the surface.

The mind is full of content: thought, images, feelings, impulses,
sensations.

Body fully attended to opens a door for joy to fly out, fill the air.

Nature abounds with joy.

Go there—

Rivers, rocks, flowers, bees, trees, ants, mountains—an ocean of
joy.

And in the natural movement of babies, and three-year old boys
and girls, and adults

who have learned how to let go.

Joy fills the moment.

THE DOOR

My son is born.

Another soul knit in the womb of a mother.

Within nine months, my wife wants a divorce, and two catastrophic terrorist strikes bring down the Twin Towers in lower Manhattan. The country falls into terror.

Though beauty lies on the other side of terror, few people can see through the burning buildings, the wreckage, and the vast fissure of fear inside their own hearts. I am no exception. But I do turn inward, descend toward my terror—not completely trapped by fear in a world filled with uncertainty. I seek the stillness deep within.

My life transforms.

Often transformation comes from a gift of betrayal, unrequited love, or some other haunting. I return to my own birth circumstances. Nothing prepares me for the initial shock of the inner journey, its complexity and depth of feeling. Fury reigns with murderous thoughts and a slow, steady, sinking into the hurt from where I observe and touch my wounds with awareness and loving kindness. As I examine my past, every joy and hurt and every turn in the road, I realize everything I experienced in my life has led me to becoming a father at forty-five years of age.

In the north, where I was born in the early spring under a hot, sticky sun and an azure sky, free-floating icebergs glided down the river in Saint John, Newfoundland, the easternmost point of

North America. Ice chunks the size of skyscrapers calved from great mother ice fields in Greenland and Iceland, the high arctic float, accompanied by loud cracking sounds, thunderous booms. These macro events mirrored my birth from a sac of warm water, thrust into the still, cool air, while an iceberg broke off, floated away, and died, a return of what had been frozen, back to the fluid sea.

Likewise, my son, cocooned in warm, womb-fluid for nine months, emerged. He is here, softly breathing, snug in the cradle of my arms as I rock him. The unity of love weaves a blanket around us. Something inside me, around the edges of my heart, begins to melt.

Absolute quiet.

Winter silence.

"Look, he's my son too," I say. "Go. Go. Just go! You haven't gone out in six months. The goddamn leaves have already fallen, Sarah! Go! Don't forget your hat. It's getting cold."

I toss my wife her hat. "I'm sure! Go. We'll be fine." I close the door, straighten the floor mat, and hang a fallen coat.

A thought rises. I hear myself mumble out loud, "First time mothers. Wow! And, she wanted two kids!"

A friend, raising four kids and still married, warned me.

"Look Seannie, you're in for a ride. Loonier than monkeys."

"Yeah, on mescaline!"

Sarah had been nuts since the moment of conception, wouldn't get any support through the whole pregnancy. I had to drag her to a group for pregnant moms at Mass General. Sat in the hospital parking lot, in my car, for three hours, waiting for her. I called my mother. "That's what love is son—*waiting*, dear, love is waiting. Often dear, it really *is* just about waiting."

The previous weekend, Sarah stumbled downstairs with Beau slung over her shoulder. "What did you do to my son?" she yelled. "What did you do? He's *bleeding!*"

She had cut her arm somehow, and there was blood on the baby's cheek, *her blood*. And she's yelling at me. *Nuts!*

I'm alone with my son for the first time.

I hear Beau; he's up. That's my boy!

What a pair of lungs. I charge upstairs, pick him up, bundle him in my arms, walk downstairs carefully. Place him on the floor. "Go ahead, crawl around little guy. You're like a fish without fins. Gotta get those arms and legs going, boy." Strange, how we talk to babies, dogs, cats, birds, squirrels, as if they know what we're saying.

"Hey, where you going? Jeez, get back over here. WOW you moved, son!"

I crawl over and pick up Beau.

He cries.

"Where do you think you're going, tiger?"

I cuddle him in my arms, whispering, "There you go, there you go." Bottle in hand. Shake drops onto my forearm. "Shit! Too cold! Milkies, milkies, milkies in a minute." A thought. *Gawd, sounds like I'm writing a bloody nursery rhyme.*

"Okay. Wait! Wait. Wait." Boil some water, stick the bottle in the water, wait twenty, thirty seconds. "Here you go, Beau!"

I almost drop him. *God, he's like a rainy-day football.* "There there, there there, there, that's good. There there, there ... there, there." I wander around the kitchen talking to Beau.

Does he even understand a word I'm saying?

I've never seen such tiny toes, like peas.

Beau poops, again.

"Goddam! Cry, crap, cry, crap, drink, cry, crap." I extend his little body, move my nose away from the smell. "Where are those diapers?" I have never changed a diaper alone. Didn't date women with kids. I can't imagine cloth diapers, my mother, four kids, no wonder, us kids. How the hell did she do it? Fathers grinding away in gray-suit land, dinner on the table every night; mothers in the '50s must have been braindead. The patron saint of mothers had to have been working twenty-four-seven.

New diaper, but Beau won't stop crying.

Wha! Wha, Whaaaaaaaaaaaaaaa!

"There, there, there, there. Stop crying."

We walk in circles. The crying won't stop, feels like five, ten, fifteen minutes.

"What's wrong with you?"

I scream at myself. *Don't, don't you dare say that, don't say that to him.* My father said that to me. I won't say it. I won't.

"You're fine. You're fine. There, there, there. Daddy's lost, Daddy's lost, Daddy's—"

Wha! Wha, Whaaaaaaaaaaaaaaaa!

Milkies, diaper, walking, burp. Burp! That's next—get a burp! But no burp! "There, there, there, that's good, there—good, good, great, great, great. That's it. We're working for a belch, Beau. Please stop crying. "What's wr—I, I think, I think, I'll put you in our bed, upstairs. That's it; that'll work! Okay, *okay*, you must stop crying."

I trip on a rainbow-bird stuffed animal.

"Goddamn it! These *toys*, everywhere!

Wha! Wha, Whaaaaaaaaaaaaaaaa! Whaaaaaaaaaaaaaaaa!

Your mother will be home soon! "Stop crying, *please!*"

He'll smell his mother's scent. Get pillows. I need big pillows.

I fluff pillows. "That's good. That's good! GOOD!"

Whaaa!

"Stop crying! I'll take you to the zoo, the Red Sox, golf, hoop. We'll kayak, mountain climb, scale rock faces, but you must stop crying. Beau, PLEASE!"

Whaaaaaaaaaaaaaaa! Whaaaaaaaaaaaaaaa! Whaaaaaaaaaaaaaaa!

"Stop! Stop crying. Stop crying! *Stop crying!* We have to stop crying."

What is wrong with him? I pick him up, put him down. I must leave, get out of this room!

GOT ... TO ... GET ... OUT ... OF ... THIS ... ROOM! ... OUT!

Whaaaaaaaaaaaaaaa! Whaaaaaaaaaaaaaaa! Whaaaaaaaaaaaaaaa!

Go in the baby's room. His room. Good! I'll go in here. Shut the door. Calm down. Calm down. That's good, calm down.

Why won't he? "Stop! Stop! *Stop crying!*"

Smash the door closed. The doorjamb buckles. "Shit!"

The handle won't turn.

I push.

Nothing.

I grab the top corner, pull at the edges with my fingers. The door snaps shut. *Oh. God! Oh, my God, I'm locked in. Locked in!* "Breathe. Breathe. Breathe."

I pull again on the top edge. The door snaps back.

"Christ! There ... has ... got ... to ... be ... a ... way ... out ... of ... here!"

"Way!" I slide my back down the wall in the baby's room and start to cry, hear myself wailing now. "Daddy didn't mean to yell. Daddy didn't mean to yell. Daddy ..."

I see the door to a closet and remember the crawl space between the master bedroom and the room I'm stuck in.

"Son, son, son. Oh, my God, son! I'm coming Beau, I'm coming! Daddy's coming!"

I kneel, creep, cross-crawl, push suitcases, swat spider webs. The closet door to the master bedroom won't open from the inside. I swirl onto my back, bend my knees, and kick the door open. Rush to my son.

Cradle Beau.

"That's it, that's it, there, there, there. No more crying. You're fine, you're fine. Daddy's here. Daddy's here. There, there. We're fine. Fine ..."

I cradle my son against my chest, which rises and falls with deep heaving breaths, just like my marriage.

Marriage can feel like war.

On the hardwood floor, I cradle Beau in my arms.

The crying stops. He blinks. Softly, gradually, he closes his eyes. I sing, whisper into his ear, *Too-ra-loo-ra-loo-ral, Too-ra-loo-ra-li.* The front door opens.

I hear Sarah's voice. Beau sleeps.

We never speak about the door.

WINTER

What happens just happens.
Yet, love
The vastness of all that exists
Nudges
Offers intimations.
Gifts given.
Signs posted.
We lack minute vision
Love is a small thing.
A whisper,
A murmur,
The slightest sound of suggestion.
Tender touch.
A season,
A winter not of discontent but discovery.
Seeds stitched somewhere long ago
Must be felt in the body.
The deep waters stir in the ice of winter.

THE GIFT

My birth father is a ghost,
A flicker in the field of my memory.
A shadow cast on the edges
Of relationship to self and others.
When he raped a woman,
His violent seed made a mother—
Mine.
Then he left town,
Gone for good,
His name unknown
But never forgotten.
The gift?
Revenge and fury need an object.
Ghosts don't qualify, so
I opened to love.

FATHER

I prepare Beau's dinner.

Try to fold him into the high chair in the kitchen. It's like wrestling a baby python—legs kick and twist, spine arches, arms wiggle and thrust upwards. He's praying feverishly to the gods.

At fifteen months old, custom-made steamed and mushed carrots and good old Gerber strained peas are his favorites, and, of course, warmed milk. The step-by-step process gives me the illusion of control, keeps me from falling from the edge of the abyss.

His mother dropped him off unexpectedly midafternoon. No reason. The bell rang, she handed him to me, mumbled something incoherent, backed away from the front step of the apartment building, flung both hands and arms into the air, then made this sound with her cheeks and mouth, a grunt-puff. There was an exhausted, pleading, crazed look on her face. Sarah is dedicated, a good mother, but she is overwrought. She looks like she's headed to the neurosurgeon or a bottle of Jack Daniels, but she wisely dropped Beau off for a spell with me.

There are many reasons why kids should have two parents in the same house.

Survival comes to mind.

"Just feed him, bathe him, read him a story. Nothing's wrong. I'll be back later. Please."

Nothing's wrong!

Other than I had reluctantly agreed to meet her divorce lawyer in two weeks to see if the guy could mediate a deal between us. In the heat of our conflict, I chose to remember why I fell in love with her in the first place.

Her overwhelm and vulnerability are palpable. *She's trusting me with Beau*, when it isn't my watch. My shoulders loosen, my fists unfurl. I pick up my son and trudge upstairs.

Boil two pots of water, not too long, pull bottle from water as soon as the bubbling begins. Peel carrots, dump carrots into small pot, mush with mush-thingy. They have tools for everything. What a country we live in.

The train rumbles down the track outside our apartment. I lift Beau onto the ledge of the window. "Twain," he screeches. "Twain, Dada! Twain!"

Beau kicks his legs and refuses to be seated back in the high chair. I hold him against my chest and feel our hearts beat together. Breathe deeply as the soft edges of dusk spread across the room. Finally, I slide the kid into the chair. He's grumpy. My girlfriend, Michelle, a mother of three, had been showing me how to finesse things, basic stuff—baby-rearing mechanics. I give Beau his food.

"Milkies!"

"No, Bodhi (his newest nickname because sometimes I feel like I'm talking to Buddha), you must eat your food first."

"Milkies! Milkies! Beau milk!"

"That's good. Milk. That *is* the word—milk." I repeat, "Mell-ka. Very good, Bodhi. Now, eat your food Daddy made, and I'll warm the milk for you. Just how you like it."

"Beau milk! Beau milk!"

I should get a clue of what's wrong here, but no. I've been feeding him in a certain order—order is *the* way—fatherhood and order.

We battle for about twenty minutes or so, which feels like three hours, back and forth, until Beau tosses his food bowl at me.

"Milkies!"

The headlights of another commuter train flood the apartment.

"Twain! Twain! Twain!"

"Take one bite of your food and you can see the next train."

You think he ate a bite? Not on your life. I don't let him see the train.

He is *pissed*! He grabs bits of pea mush and carrots and spasmodically tosses the food, screaming.

"Milkies! Milkies! Milkies!"

I do what any hopelessly exhausted and defeated father would do. I slump down onto the kitchen floor mumbling to myself.

In desperation, I decide to call Michelle for girlfriend input.

She answers. *Thank God.*

"I don't know what to do. He won't eat his food. He keeps screaming for milk. The kid won't eat. I made the food the way I always make it."

She laughs. "Try giving him the milk first."

"But I read in a book you are not supposed . . ."

"Just try it."

"One minute." I put the phone on the counter and hand Beau his Snoopy sippy cup. *Boom.* The kid sucks back a few mouthfuls, then begins to eat his food. And he grins at me—actually, grins—like a friend might when they've got one over on you.

"He's friggin' smiling!"

"Honey, you can't learn about parenting in books. Things change constantly, evolve constantly. He's growing."

I hang up, relieved.

JOURNEY

There's a golden string
Made of finest silk

Woven from the tip
Of an angel's wing

Fastened to the back
Of my fierce heart

When I cut the chord
The angel reaches down

And ties a knot
I rise

Stumbling into Joy

STRONGEST MAN IN THE WORLD

As I stare at my son, I think of Jim Thorpe, the Native American from Oklahoma, who was considered the strongest man in the world in the 1920s after winning both the Decathlon and Pentathlon for America at the Stockholm Olympics. Amazingly, many of his records stood until the 1980s. The Sac and Goos Native American went on to become a star in professional football and baseball. In the 1960s, the sport writers of America voted Jim the greatest athlete of the half-century.

At the peak of his athletic prowess, scientists decided to test Jim Thorpe's strength versus a toddler's with an unusual experiment. He was to spend four days mirroring everything a specific toddler did. If the kid squatted to play with blocks for ten minutes, so did Jim. If the kid did somersaults or ran around wildly, so did Jim. The scientists planned to observe for four days and judge who had more endurance. The study was called off because Jim Thorpe quit after just four hours. He was exhausted.

THE MILKSHAKE

In grade three, Beau came home rattled, upset about a kid in gym class bullying a friend of his.

"He keeps picking on him, Daddy."

"Why?'"

"Doesn't like him. And Tommy is small. The other kid pushes him down to the floor all the time."

"The gamer kid?"

"Yup. Tommy. He's my friend."

"Well, you have options, Beau."

"Like what?" Beau cocks his head.

Beau is a big, gentle boy, second tallest in his class. Like most boys, he connects with his friends in a bump-up-against each other way—grab an arm, jostle one another standing in line, wrestle. It's a good-natured, healthy way to explore their physical selves and bond.

This is a tough one for me. Parents and school administrators, society itself, have become so protective and fearful that kids can barely do anything physical. Touch a friend, slap him on the back in the hallway walking to the next class—any kind of roughhousing—gets shut down immediately.

But bullying is bullying, been around a long time.

"What did you do to a bully, Dad?"

Young boys tend to see their dads as indestructible super-heroes. That is, until they become teenagers, spread their wings, and flex their muscles.

"Stayed away from them!" I laugh.

"But what if you can't, Dad?

"Punch him in the face." The speed my response blurts from my mouth startles both of us. I pause, breathe, collect myself. "Well, let's look for some options. What could you do?"

"Tell the teacher, but then I'm a tattle-tale!"

"Hmmm."

"I could go get the teacher, 'cause he wasn't there when Billy pushed Tommy down, but we're not allowed to leave the gym."

"You could just ignore it."

"I don't like that." Beau forms a fist with his fingers—a seven-year-old with cocked fists the size of small apples.

"Your mother would say to stay out of this, Beau."

Shyly, he pushes me for something different. "But I'm asking *you*, Dad."

"I could teach you The Milkshake."

The pupils of his eyes widen. "The Milkshake?"

"The Devil taught it to me."

"The Devil?"

"Yep. Tough Romanian kid, Patty Saray. We called him the Devil. I grew up with him, back home. He taught me The Milkshake when Rocky Leduc took my track and field medals and tossed them down the sewer at recess."

"Wow. That was mean! Were you mad?"

"Yes, but he was three years older and crazy, so I just stayed away from him the best I could."

"What about The Milkshake?"

"He was too big, so I waited after school, near the back steps, and belted him in the head with my hockey stick."

"Dad!"

"Well, Chateauguay was a rough place, Beau."

"Did you get in trouble?"

"Nope, just two black eyes from Rocky Leduc. But he left me alone after that."

"Can you show me The Milkshake?"

"Sure." I demonstrate standing, slightly crouched for thrust, legs staggered. "The key is to grab the other guy with all your force. With both hands, grab him by his shirt at the center of his chest, twist, tighten, and pull. Then push. Pull, push, pull, push. You see? Shake him back and forth very, very fast, four or five times, like a milkshake. Try it."

Beau grabs my shirt and we play, refine the move.

"What happens?"

"The kid gets so dizzy that he crumples to the floor and can't get up."

"His legs don't work?"

"Yup."

Beau went out to play in the park.

A couple years later, same kids, the Billy and Tommy thing. No call from the school, but Beau sheepishly says to me one night, while devouring homemade spaghetti, "The Milkshake really works, Daddy."

Apparently, my gentle son broke up another bullying incident by introducing Billy to The Milkshake.

"He just crunched on the floor, Dad. Couldn't get up, just like you said!"

Stumbling into Joy

RED MIST

The attorney asked Sarah to step out of the room.

Reluctantly, she did.

"Look, Mr. Leclaire, we have an open wallet on this case." The man in the smart blue suit sat at the head of his boardroom table and smirked. If he hadn't smirked, I might have let the comment tumble to the floor where it belonged. Friends had told me not to take a meeting with my estranged wife and her divorce attorney without having my own lawyer in the room. But cash was tight, and I wanted to avoid a costly court battle over custody.

I knew that fathers rarely win decent rights to their children in the courts. The open wallet was a jab, trying to intimidate me. Sarah's father was a senior partner in a prestigious Boston law firm.

I speak deliberately.

"Where I come from, we don't threaten people we don't know."

The attorney, Marcus, or Chad, or something, stiffens. "It is not a threat. I am simply stating the facts, sir."

This guy has fancy top-floor offices. I gaze out the window, stand, walk around the table, and extend my hand. As the lawyer lifts his arm, I grab him by his shirt at the center of his chest, twist, and thrust his body into the air. Two quick steps and his face smears the window.

"Doubt you'd bounce from this high up."

Moments can change a person's life. One of my favorite coaching clients calls moments like this the "red mist." I've had a handful of red-mist moments over the decades, but I'm a peaceful man now.

The room becomes still like an empty church.

I drop the attorney to the floor.

He bounces.

I open the boardroom door and walk by my ex.

"See you in court."

WILD

Up an old logging road, steep incline, climbing a fallen fir in the Hoh River rainforest.

A gap for the sky. A foot bridge to cross the mountain creek. A sensation of awe. Light pours in, vast quiet among old hemlocks draped with moss and lichen, looming granite cliffs. A stand of soaring spruce, sequoia seeded when Jesus walked the earth.

Now wild, off-the-map, off-line, deeply connected.

Trusting light, and the face in the pool of icy water at my feet. A wolf howls.

INDIVIDUATION

Begins
With a soul
Knit in the warm
Wet womb of the
World.

Baby
Burst forth
Into a cold
Spinning planet
Alone.

Born
Falling through
Space and time
Single in the
Cosmos.

Searching
For the imprint
Of its own
Magnificent
Form.

COLD WAR

Over breakfast she talks
About bad weather in Florida,
Organic cat food, and
"I didn't know Destiny's Child
was Beyonce!"
He sips coffee. "Hmm."

"How's your toast, honey?"
"What?"
"Your toast?"
"It's toast."
"I think I'll get a squash."
"What?"

"Squash for tonight's dinner
With the hotel scrod
And those red-skinned potatoes
That you like."
"Hmpf."
I think it might rain today."

His eyes on the plate,
Not a moment passes between them.
"When's the game this afternoon?"
"Two."
Some men enjoy the call to war,
and their women pray
They won't come back.

DICK THEORY

1
Don't know I am acting
like a dick.

2
Know I am acting
like a dick, a lot.

3
Act like a dick,
sometimes.

4.
Am learning, slowly
how to use my dick
wisely.

BABY JESUS

I wanted my son to see Baby Jesus in the crèche. We'd talked about the carpenter's kid from Nazareth most of December. My three-year-old son asks some doozy questions: How could he be God's only son? Could he fly like the angels? Why is his birthday on Santa's big day? How come we can't see him if Baby Jesus is always here with us?

When I was a kid, I wore out the neighborhood asking such questions, so much so that every adult on Edward Street called me Mr. How Come. I can hear my mother and father rolling in their graves laughing and thinking, "What goes around comes around."

On Christmas Eve, driving to get my son at his mother's, I'm aware of the heavy sadness I feel. This year, Beau's with me for Christmas Eve and Christmas morning till ten.

I pull into the driveway. My boy jumps in the backseat, bundled, beaming, breathless, ready for Santa's imminent arrival.

No matter how clear I am that his mother made the right choice when she left, not only for her but also for me, holidays are hard for me. They are even more difficult because I can still make the mistake of seeing my strong emotion for something other than what it is—changing weather.

"What's wrong, Daddy?" my son asks. Not much escapes his attention.

"Daddy's just tired," I respond, trying to sound more cheerful.

"Are we going to see Baby Jesus today, Daddy?"

I had told Beau we'd go see Baby Jesus after we'd read the Christmas story for the zillionth time. My son's taste for things spiritual is diverse. A tiny bronze statue of Ganesh, the Hindu elephant god, rests atop his door jamb, removing all obstacles; a stone Buddha sits on his small writing desk, giving clarity of mind; a Zen meditation cushion is on the floor of his room, which he pouts on during time-outs; and a picture of Baby Jesus is by his bed, which keeps him safe from bad dreams. He's just recently begun to dream and become worried about safety. So anytime we talk about angels or another god, he bugs me until I get him some figure, picture, or symbol of the being for our safety. "Yes, yes. We'll go visit Baby Jesus tonight at Father Austin's church," I assure Beau. I can't say it is *our* church because we don't go more than on holidays, but Beau knows I love Jesus and talk with him often.

"The reason we can't see him is because he's inside our hearts, right, Daddy?" He presses a mitten into his chest.

"Yes, in our hearts." I glance out the driver's window. There's only a scattering of snow on the ground, which makes it not really feel like Christmas.

"So we're going to see the Baby Jesus?"

"Later, Beau. Please stop!" I hate it when the emotional weather socks in and I'm in such a mood. But hating it doesn't make the mood go away. So I bring my attention to my breath, feel the heavy feeling in my chest, breathe in and out mindfully. My shoulders let go. We drive in silence, and it begins to snow lightly.

After dinner, we drive about a mile to the church to see Baby Jesus. The houses in the neighborhood twinkle with anticipation of Santa's visit tonight. In the church parking lot, Beau leaps from the car, barely waiting for it to stop, and charges toward the crèche. It seems strange that no one is around.

Walking toward the crèche, I have that warm feeling you get when a cherished memory begins to arise in your awareness. My mind drifts to my father, mother, and three sisters gathered around our cut-out crèche, the six of us planted knee-deep in snow a few feet from our front porch, caroling with neighborhood teenagers.

"Come on, Daddy!" Beau calls, as he slides on ice in front of the crèche, tumbles into a hay bale, then pops up unhurt and stares into the scene. There are three wise men riding camels, a magnificent star-bright, a cow, horse, donkey, hens, even a duck and two intrepid mice, but no Baby Jesus lying in the manger.

You can't really know what a three-year-old having a full tantrum is really like until you've lived through the experience. "Of course there's no Baby Jesus. He comes Christmas day, not Christmas Eve," I think in utter disbelief at my miscalculation. You would think that after years of exposure to the religious rigor of an Irish Catholic mother and the confraternity of Christian Doctrine, I'd have had that simple fact hardwired.

Now, I'm not breathing.

"Where's Baby Jesus! I want Baby Jesus!" Beau yells, insistently.

"Daddy made a mistake. He comes tomorrow, Beau," I admit, trying to calm him.

"I want to see Baby Jesus now!" Beau screams in fury. The lungs on healthy three-year olds are powerful beyond measure as they have not been socialized to suppress fury.

If my son's arms were wrapped tightly around his chest in full pouting mode, I could just bundle him up and whisk him to safety, meaning anyplace where the good people of Concord wouldn't think I was torturing him. But his arms are cutting the night air like slashing blades of the Hindu goddess Kali, as tears stream down his red cheeks.

"Baby Jesus, Baby Jesus, now!" he yells again. Across the street, house lights come on, and a car slows to see what the ruckus is about.

I try to grab Beau but slip on the ice and crack the back of my skull, which dulls the high-pitch sound of my boy's angry crying. Finally, I get him in my arms, but nothing can console him. He's totally pissed, and I don't blame him. I feel like a fool in every way imaginable. My boy's flailing away on my left shoulder, screaming bloody murder, and I'm navigating packed ice as I move toward the car. I try to place him in the car seat; controlling him is impossible.

I'd read in a parenting book about dealing with high-octane kids that when they have a tantrum you should let them expend their energy. Not control them, but simply provide a safe container. The suggestion must have sunk in somewhat because I close the car door and watch in amazement as my boy bounces off the backseat repeatedly, then levitates, and throws his thirty-five-pound body from side to-side against the car's interior like a rubber ball, all the while offering the world his powerful chant: "Baby Jesus, now, now, now!"

I don't know how long he continues. It feels like eternity. When he stops moving, I open the door, lift him into my arms, and plunk down on the snowbank in front of the car for a few minutes. We sit side by side under the starry night sky, and my son whispers, "I'm sorry, Daddy." I finally breathe again, and choke on my own tears.

"It was Daddy's mistake. We'll come back tomorrow on Baby Jesus's birthday.

"No, he's here *now*, Daddy." Beau points upward into the dark night.

An imperfect father and his son seated perfectly quiet in the snow under a shooting star.

BANTER

"Is yours still dragging her feet?"
"There are claw marks on their front door,
And she doesn't realize how she sees
So much backwards and upside down."
"What about that poet the Cherubim Council assigned you?"
"I hate poets!"
"Now, now, we're—"
"He's as sensitive as the tip of a fly rod; he senses us talking!"
"No!"
"Yeah, he can and—"
"The guy thinks he's an Apache."
"An Indian?"
"In Boston!"
"He gets writing and starts screaming for me to show myself!"
"What?"
"He wants to fight!"
"No!"
"Yeah! I'm telling you, poets!"
"Figures!"

PROMISE

Love wants to feed
Love wants to be fed
The circle complete

Two people rooted
Under the asphalt
of heaven

A circumference
With no center

THE BOXER

My son, a grown man now, made me a father, each sweet, steady step of the way.

The tenderness deepens.

He taught me how to love.

Way back when he was a toddler, we used to have the nightly ritual: dinner, tubby, teddy, story, sleep. A sweet cuddle with his rainbow blankie in the big blue chair.

One night, I hear Beau in the bathtub splashing about, spraying his plastic water pistol everywhere. I call for him to get out. He does, but begins to doddle down the hall, puddles of water on the hardwood floor. I chase him, and with both my hands, I tap and push his butt into his bedroom.

"Come on. Need to get jammies on, read a story, sleepy-time, Mister!"

He turns, butt-naked with a boner like boys get. He puts his hands on his hips, and says, "Daddy, there is no pushing at school, and there's no pushing at home."

Pushing? He was three years old and teaching me not to push.

As he grew, I grew up.

There were moments when he was a certain age that I *re-lived* being that very same age. Unfinished business rose in me, which happens to all parents; we just need to notice.

By his ninth birthday, Beau was convinced he wanted to be a boxer. Nagged me for a pair of boxing gloves for months. I finally caved, got him the gloves. He slept with the damn things. Kept popping me left and right, nonstop.

"Teach me, Dad. Teach me how, Dad."

I decline.

"You were a tough guy, Dad. You knocked out a Golden Gloves champ!"

I had mistakenly told him a story. Kids have long memories.

"In a street fight, son. That's much different."

"But you boxed! I wanna box. Be a champ."

"There are no upper middle-class boxing champs, son."

"Why not?"

I tried logic. "Not angry enough. The working poor make the best boxers."

"Were you angry, Dada?"

"Some, yeah, well, a lot."

"I wanna box."

I rent the DVD, the documentary about all the guys who fought Muhammud Ali.

"Daddy, how come that man can't speak right?"

"Because Ali hit him in the head nine hundred times one night. That's what boxing is, son, getting hit and hitting back, faster and harder."

My boy is tender, sweet; no animosity in him. But he wants to box.

We went to the park. I got on my knees. We boxed.

I popped him once in the chest. It hurt. He began to cry. That was the plan. I stopped boxing in its tracks.

There are enough men beating each other up in the world.

My son is in college now. He's got a big brain, kind heart, and his bell has never been rung by extreme force.

THE JOB

A gunman walks into a popular restaurant chain in town. Shoots and kills two waiters and three customers. No reason. Some of us have always been crazy.

My roommate Brof reads me the story. "Some maniac shot up the Keg n' Cleaver last night!" We're at college, second year, and our money has run out. Badly need a job. I grab the paper. "Let me see that."

"Are you nuts, Seannie?"

"Not like the shooter. They'll need waiters, man!"

The following Wednesday, I drive to the Keg and apply for a job as a waiter. An assistant manager fidgets, talks without pause. I eyeball a few bullet holes by the bar.

"You heard, right?"

"I know. That's why I'm here."

"Well, our manager, Bill, will be back at four."

"I'll wait outside."

A man drives up, jumps out of his Jeep, and walks in the side door of the building. I take a few steps over and lean on his Jeep. Seems like a take-charge, boss-type guy.

Twenty minutes later, Bill opens the main door to the restaurant. "You want a job?"

"I figured you'd be short of staff."

He nods. "Can you start now?"

I nod.

"Seen some action?"

"Yup. My roommate said I'd have to wash dishes before getting to be a waiter."

"Not now. You start waiting, tonight."

We shake hands.

TWO GUYS TALKING
IN A COFFEE SHOP

Completely insane
Really?
The platform
We can monitor
Mailboxes
A strength of ours
Can't remove people though
Or the whole platform might
Go away—
What?
The bedrock data
We ignore that
What?
The domain add
Google says—
Who?
Google, where?
Mountain View
What?
We're
Pushing
Burning
Driving

Accelerating
A cash flow crunch coming
Maybe downsizing
People?
Why people?
We need faster activation
Mode
A mode
Yeah!
A strength of ours
Launch point
What?
Launch Point!
Yeah.
I know them
Really insane!
Superfast
Mode—
What?
Mode
Lean, agile.
Ah, yeah!
Insane

Stumbling into Joy

But so much stress
The system?
No
People.
Yeah.

Launch point?
Awesome
Completely insane
Yeah!

And there are women
Who have sex
With these guys.

PACE

Speed is revered
in a googly world.

But can you see small things
At high speed?
Love is a small thing.

The way tide and dusk
Move in and out each day.
Water and light know slow too.

What a world
We are allowing
These technologists

To generate here,
Hell on earth.

THE WAY IT IS

In days-gone-by, when we had a perplexing problem, a dilemma, or just needed someone to listen, we'd reach out to a close friend or trusted family member, or maybe a priest, a wise neighbor, or even the local bartender. Genuine giving and receiving occurred.

Then psychology came, therapists with methods and modalities, and the so-called spiritual gurus, then the coaches. Some trained up the yin-yang, others with not much training. Probably better they went to therapy for a decade or so before they started coaching.

My friends are farmers and fishermen, artists and scientists, and an unusual gathering of men who meet Saturday mornings in Maynard, Massachusetts. These people are gentle souls, for the most part, but they do not suffer fools. And they know how to listen. My friends tend not to give advice. They listen, and sometimes offer a profound or startling question. We rely on each other.

Nowadays, everything moves so fast, most people have little leisure time. Most people are isolated and alienated from themselves and each other.

I wouldn't go so far as to say that we—this culture of speed and efficiency— have commodified friendship. It is more like we have forgotten how to talk to each other as friends and how to listen. I think coaches can be useful. But if you have a coach, and your coach is your only friend, your only trusted confidant, then I suggest you take a hard look at that choice.

Life is too short to have people you pay as "friends."

Extend yourself, make a real friend, risk being vulnerable, trust one person. There is deep power in vulnerability. Rilke said it best.

"Perhaps everything terrible is in its deepest being something helpless that wants help from us." We are all helpless at some point.

Be someone's close friend.

COIN TOSS

One side,
Pride

The other,
Shame

Either way

Nothing
But ego
Currency

MARKS

My son is failing school.

His mom is at her wits' end.

Ds and Fs, grade nine.

Our son is bored to death, which can happen to bright kids.

His mom and I do not pressure Beau.

"I am not going to be a bloody helicopter parent!" she said.

Beau gets a pass that way, unlike many of his friends. But failing in school closes doors.

He isn't adjusting to high school well. I had the same problem and never did pull my socks up. I was allowed to cruise by because I was a basketball star. I had special privileges, which worked *against* me when I graduated into the real world. The world gave me my real schooling, soon enough.

I want my son to understand. But how much can you really pass on to your kids? Some values, like honesty, punctuality, respect, and kindness. Beau is already kind; he is just bored. Boredom is a lack of attention.

I need to give him something to attend to. I haven't given many father speeches, but I give him this one:

"Look, son, it is a game. Do you hear me? A game! You are losing the game. Give them what they want, and then you get to do what you want."

The ballistic tone and the stillness work. Sometimes, rarely, a father, can use silence and fury in cahoots. I knew I had him when he said, "Well, not everyone is like a US Navy Seal who wants to win the race up every bloody mountain, Dad!"

I sat still and silent. I remember smiling inside.

"The choice is yours."

He drilled down, gave the teachers what they wanted, and graduated magna cum laude.

A well-timed paternal slap helped.

BANKER

Worry is the interest
We pay on fear.

Don't compound that shit
Here.

RING OF FIRE

People, places, and things
Are triggers,

But never the cause
Of our pain

Draw a circle,
A ring of fire around
Yourself.

Burn that stuff up
What's left?

Love

THE SCOOTER

I'm seated in my car in a Toys R Us parking lot, having a mini-panic attack, still breathing, but jumpy and unfocused. My mother would have called the state "having ants in my pants." I can't seem to get myself to drive to daycare, pick up my son, go home, make supper, and give him the gift I bought for his fifth birthday, a Star Wars Darth Vader scooter.

Once home in the living room of my apartment with my son, I'm anxious and upset. The reason for this doesn't dawn on me until too late. He wants me to *assemble* the scooter.

I dump the contents of the Darth Vader box onto the hardwood floor and watch apprehensively as the parts fly out. Some memory presses for my attention. Since my son was born, I've been reliving repressed events and incidents from my childhood. Even though I've gotten used to it, the whole process is eerie, troubling. It's a gift really, but it doesn't feel like one right now.

Sitting there on my couch, I suddenly hear my father's distant voice saying, "You've got two thumbs for fixing things, boy." He revered tools and could make anything with his hands. I could do anything with a basketball, golf ball, or soccer ball. I wasn't comfortable using tools, and my dad didn't give me much support for using them. His comments could make me feel like an imbecile. He wasn't mean, just not much of a teacher.

Glaring at the parts wrapped in plastic bags and the semi-assembled scooter, I blurt out, "I don't have proper tools for this.

We'll have to wait."

"But, Dad, you've got tools in the orange toolbox. I'll get it. I want to ride my scooter now!" He is charging down the hallway.

Now is my son's favorite word. He thumps into the room, toolbox in hand. I'm sitting there trying to get the stem of the damn thing into the front wheel base. "Try turning it around,' Beau suggests.

The kid's right. The thing fits.

I attempt to put a few brackets together, but a screw the size of a nanobot falls out of my fingertips and lands in the seam of the hardwood floor. I clench my stomach and jaw and hear myself make an odd sound like a trapped animal dying.

My boy hands me a pen from my desk and says, "Flip it up from the hole in the wood with this, Dad!" I feel an impulse to scream, but instead, after a few long seconds, retrieve the tiny screw.

"See!" He proudly acknowledges his solution and my effort. Then he pats me on the back.

I turn a black plastic thingy that is supposed to hook, and then complain, "We need to get better tools to do this. I just can't get this. Get Patrick, Blase; they can do it. You can ride the scooter next time we're together."

"Dad, we can do it! Look!" my son shouts encouragingly as he points to the picture on the box. "Put it upside down, Dad." I turn the bracket and easily slip in the stem.

At that moment, I hear my father in the room with us, right beside me on the couch, just breathing, not saying a word. Here with his adopted son and grandson, who he never met, who just turned five and wants to ride his new scooter now. I loosen my jaw. A few tears slide down my cheeks.

My son grabs his scooter from me and says, "Cool! We did it, Dad. See! Works great!" He rolls around on it.

I am exhausted, beyond belief.

My son utterly fills me up and depletes me, daily. Many parents think they should suppress their old hurts from childhood and get on with things. I found that strategy doesn't work well. There's a healing that happens when you meet whatever rises from your muddy past with honesty, mercy, and vulnerability, especially right in front of your kids. I sensed my son appreciated my awkwardness and the chance to help me do something he wanted done.

While I stand by the front window watching Beau glide gleefully down the driveway on his new scooter, I smile. The memory of my father's harsh words dissolves.

LESSON

I have learned to trust
That the gods work

More truly and clearly
Through other people,

Than through myself.
Some call this
"Humility."

Humble has nothing

To do with it.
More like
Acceptance.

FAST

We dance to machine gun fire
Words, words, words
Worming, whirling, whizzing
Lines of bullets
Tracer fire
Day and night on the flat screen
Words
And pictures.
      War on the mind
Missiles
Now
Shoot back.
Media
Fast.

.

MY TREE

Willow
Water's weeping friend
Wind's courtesan
Whirling
Pressed by afternoon storms
She rings like tiny bells.
Rooted in earth's sorrow,
After rain her branches resemble tears
Swaying, stretching, waving
Turning with the seasons,
My tree
Stronger than the oak.

UNITY

Coffee shop cups clatter
A rush of steam

Funky blues on the radio
Front door opens

Cold breeze and a mother enter
Barista whips another latte

What else could possibly happen
Unity grounds a world of form

The eye of God is the same eye
I am

Only sensation now
Now aliveness

Aliveness abounds
I am happiness itself

PRAYER

Fill my heart with love
Mind with clarity
Soul with fire

Body with ease
Spirit with courage
That's pretty much it

Oh, and could you give
The technologists
Just, *just*, a bit of wisdom

WHOLENESS

I'm alone now.

Aloneness is easeful, but periodically the longing arises to be with another, to cherish another, to be cherished; to enjoy a tender touch, holding hands, sharing wit and ideas, giving a shoulder to cry on, cuddling on the couch, uproarious laughter, a mate with whom to share a big win at work. Someone to love and support.

When I sit with the longing, a deeper longing arises that has nothing to do with another person. Wholeness itself seeks us.

It is unusual for two whole people to meet, but it can happen, like real love.

Rare and beautiful.

ACCEPTANCE

What is coming
to you is coming to you.

What is not coming
to you is not coming to you.

Why worry?

DOWNTOWN

I drank till my face hit the pavement
and did not understand,
that years of sharpness had sent
the lack of a caring hand.

I stretched my dreams for dinner,
on a cold and creeping day.
The priests, they shaped a sinner—
with blood in my eyes, I prayed.

SWIM

Some days you wake up.
Tossed into a furious river,
Rapid whitewater,
Salmon time.
If you do not swim you go over the falls.
No one survives the fall.
Don't take it personally.
It's just the current of the day.
Swim like a motherfucker.
And keep your head above water.

HOMELESS

I see him standing by the chess tables in Washington Square Park.

Not like one of the chess hustlers I normally see there, who are drug addicts and really good at chess. This man is different, and he is shivering.

I am drawn to connect and help street people, but sometimes I use a kind of boot camp approach. Recently, a man slumped on a subway bench and I got into a doctrinal-level discussion about Job's plight in the Bible. A story about the testing of Job's faith. I did not raise the topic, Victor did. His perspective and interpretation was provocative and lucid.

Often, homeless people are drug addicts, petty thieves and hustlers, or ne'er-do-wells; sometimes, mentally disturbed beyond repair. Others are just plain nasty buggers I'd beat with a baseball bat, if I had to. And then, there's Sarafez, a.k.a. Surfi. He's standing in the park staring at the wet grass on a cold February morning.

"Are you homeless?"

"Yes."

"Why are you homeless? Do you not have any skills?"

He explains that he earns six dollars an hour teaching chess to NYU students who wander into the park and that his work permit will not come until June. Surfi makes about $550 a month teaching chess. For eighteen months he has fought in the system to get refugee status. Legal aid handled his case for free. Almost two years homeless.

I tell Surfi I know some Sanskrit, a language I knew he'd know, and we chant a prayer together. He begins to cry. I have not seen a homeless street person cry in many years.

"You are a kind man, but your Sanskrit is terrible!" We laughed. We agree I will pay him $10 an hour to learn proper enunciation on Tuesday mornings in the park. Surfi can't work legally for four more months. Bone-cold months. He sleeps on the A-train subway at night, two, three hours max. He eats once every three days and "showers" standing up in bathrooms. When he can, he reads and studies at the main library. Surfi is a PhD economist but cannot work. He knows no one in the city. I ask him why he doesn't sleep in the homeless shelters. He gives me a strange look, one you see in people's faces when they are deciding whether to trust you or not. I see this look a lot in the executive leadership workshops I do.

Surfi takes off his winter jacket. Lifts up his shirt, exposes a belly covered with nasty bed bug bites.

"I had to fill out a 35-page document to get into a shelter that gave me this. I will not do that, Sean; I will not do that again, ever!"

After I stop crying, we play a game of chess. I lose.

Surfi helps me refine my Sanskrit pronunciation and improve my chess game. I organize a cohort of friends and clients who contribute the funds required to jump-start Surfi's life. He's off the streets, happy, still playing and teaching chess. We are friends.

During Ramadan, Sarafez said to me,

"Allah says that to save one life is to save all humanity."

THE MIRROR

I am aware
There is more luxury
In my New York apartment
Bathroom than in billions of lives.
Cold and hot running water, flushing toilet,
Lavender soap, plush towels, soft bum wipe,
Medicines, skin creams, and such.
I could go on:
A toilet plunger for when things
Back up, a large bathtub, shampoo, a candle, toothpaste,
A clear mirror, Arnica, Calendula, Oral B's gliding floss,
An extra dental floss, a vibrating toothbrush,
A porcelain sink, bandages, a bottle of ginger massage oil.
When I travel to many countries, and parts of Hell's Kitchen,
The slow-to-gentrify Irish neighborhood
Where I live in New York,
I can't help but notice that people do not have teeth.
The mirror reflects my image—
And the dim light in the eyes says:
Complaint lives in the suburbs of God.

Stumbling into Joy

POLARITY

Friends ask me, "Why do you coach corporate types?"

The word *type* prompts me to reach for my broadsword. I have been known to swing the sharp blade on occasion.

One man, a community activist, offers a clear image. "Isn't it like pissing into the wind, Sean?"

After I stop laughing, I said, "Yes, Bill, I get wet once in a while, no doubt! But here's the thing, man. I'd rather work on the inside and get these folks to wake up to the real level of fear they swim in, get them to make small changes in how they think and lead that can have significant impact on many people's lives. Some of my clients are responsible for tens of thousands of employees."

"But they are destroying the planet!"

"Look Bill, you stand on the sidewalk with your cardboard signs throwing stones at skyscrapers. They don't even know you are there."

We went for a long walk, and the conversation dropped into the misuse of technology, the idiocy of technologists, the fault lines of neoliberalism, how global companies hold their executives hostage through "payouts," and alien work status restrictions. "They are well-paid slaves, and they don't even realize it." Bill is a tough nut, fiercely dedicated to citizen rights.

The thing about liberals is that they actually think their heart-felt perspective is right. And the thing about conservatives is . . . Well, you get the problem.

Polarities like global/local, shareholder/society, centralization/decentralization. And polarities in our minds like scarcity/abundance, chaos/order, and fear/love. Polarities are woven into our culture and minds. Polarities don't listen.

It seems to me that an aware person, a conscious leader, whether on the front lines of the activist cause, in a senate seat, or at the boardroom table, is a person who can see, hear, understand, and empathetically consider multiple perspectives of any given context. But many leaders, like my friend, filter everything through their own position. And any position is simply hardened perspective. At best, they do either/or: it's either this or that. This is limited, dualistic thought.

Real leaders build bridges.

LISTEN

A person speaks to us,
We think we are listening.
We are not, we are in
Our own story.

We hear the words,
And go immediately to
Memory, the bank
Of our own experience.

Listening occurs only
When we are receptive.
Receptivity requires
An empty mind.

THIRST

Even as the meeting begins,
My throat dry, in need of water.
I'm standing inside towering glass and corporate steel.
On top of downtown Manhattan, the Statue of Liberty
Like a toy on the majestic Hudson River.
The CEO appears worried,
They often do.
After years away from the corporate game,
My heart now open for business,
I bow, extend a hand;
I've learned to listen.
We are not the water we swim in,
Only the water we drink.

RAIN

A homeless guy called John said to me, "Dog spelled backward is God, so dog must be man's best friend, right?"

We never know what people are thinking, reflecting upon. I have a hard time imagining John on his dumpster dives, looking for food and having that curious thought.

In New York, where I live, many upper middle-class citizens treat their dogs much better than the homeless. Why is that?

I'll be strolling down any sidewalk in Manhattan and pass a woman or man fussing with their pet poodle; the dog wears a plastic rain jacket and little shoes on its poodle paws. I'm not joking. Sometimes these dogs have hats. Steps away there's a man, usually black, curled in an alcove, trying to evade the rain. The pet owner does not see the homeless man.

Riding in a limousine to the Munich airport after an important meeting, we're on our way to another grinder session in Paris. Such is the way of global leaders; they move, quickly. I'm his executive coach and not caught up with the twists and turns of our day, so far. I do my best to help, but it is all theater to me. The stage, scenery, players, and plot are more or less the same everywhere I go. Good people working in corrupt corporate cultures, trying to find a unifying common purpose beyond merely profit. For the most part they don't.

It is rare to meet a global leader who has touched a deeper

sense of their own purpose and brought that power into an organization in order to serve customers, stakeholders, employees, and society. Truly rare.

"I need to drive down on this, find a way to leverage the team more effectively, Sean."

"How could the team's purpose help?"

"Not sure. Things are crazy right now—the new CEO, his stupid play-to-win credo. I feel like I'm in bloody college again."

"What'd you like about college, Alan?" The client furiously flips through slides.

"What?"

"College…"

"Ahhh, astrophysics, the women, and playing hockey— intramural."

"I thought you played hoop?"

No, that was Mike."

"Right."

"I need to work on this?"

"Why not just have a conversation? Let's come up with a few good questions for the room, and we'll start there?"

Clients over-rely on decks and data, so much focus on damage control.

"Close your laptop. What do you notice?"

"Where?"

"As we're driving."

"Signs, the highway, cars, a semi-trailer, it is starting to rain, I hate rain." We pass another stone bridge. Underneath there are people, kids, moms, dads, a dog or two, whole families. Under the bridges, in tents.

"What else?"

"Jesus, man, I have to prepare. We need to motivate, inspire these new people on the team!"

"I bet the Syrians could use some inspiration right now."

"What?"

"And, probably shoes. Maybe jobs in your warehouses. Don't you have warehouses here?"

"Yeah, but…" Suddenly, Alan sees the people under the bridges.

"Refugees, gawd, they're everywhere."

"Doesn't your CEO know Merkel?"

"I think so."

It didn't take much.

Alan asked his new team this question: "What would it look like if we expand the use of our purpose to include refugees?"

The program was simple. Teach them English, then hire workers for warehouses: forklift drivers, stackers, electricians, inventory clerks, truck drivers. Twenty-seven Syrians who were homeless and lost, fathers, mothers, sons, and daughters living in tents under bridges, now work for a global shoe company in Germany because Alan had the courage to take an action.

He asked the question; his team did the rest.

New York, Munich, Tel Aviv, Singapore, Toronto, Paris, all fine cities, filled with immigrants who could be given a real shot at a life.

I'll never get to the people with their well-dressed poodles. I've seen enough upper middle-class New Yorkers cleaning up their dog shit on the sidewalks and enough black men begging for one lifetime. But I still meet the Alan's of the world, and they help me remember why I do what I do.

A rich man is just a poor man with money.

DING, DING, DING

Our universe is structured in threes.

Space: length, width, depth.

Time: past, present, future.

Literature: beginning, middle, end.

The main properties of subatomic particles: charge, mass, spin. The building blocks of atoms: proton, electron, neutron. The states of matter: solid, liquid, gas. Three types of massive objects: planets, stars, galaxies.

Three kingdoms: animal, mineral, vegetable. Religions: the trinity of Vishnu, Shiva, and Brahmin; Judaism's: Passover, Shavuot, and Sukkot; the Father, Son, and Holy Ghost. The Bible is riddled with threes.

In sports: the triple axel, three-pointers, and a hat trick.

Advertising jingles: "snap, crackle, pop."

The Nina, the Pinta, and the Santa Maria; the Three Musketeers; Olympic bronze, silver, and gold.

And who can forget the Three Stooges or the rhythm of our jokes: A Rabbi, a Priest, and an Irishman walk into a bar.

When I work with clients, I engage body, mind, and spirit. And that approach has made all the difference. If one of the three is off-kilter or out-of-whack—that three-word phrase—then the other two also tend to be.

At a lovely manor in rural France, I offered a "rhythm of three" talk to a global leadership team working in the life sciences.

"Have you noticed that I tend to introduce new concepts in three ways?" A few people nod.

"The world and humans are structured in threes. If you want to flow, tap into the rhythm of three. Pay attention, you'll see what I'm saying is true." The room went silent.

Although all clients supposedly turned off their phones during the workshop, just as I ended my talk, someone's cell phone chimed, three times. People's jaws dropped, and nervous laughter filled the room.

Ding, ding, ding.

TRANSFORMATION

The tree is more present than humans.
Sensitive to change, she prepares,
Stops making green leaves.

Her true colors come forth.
She knows how to be.
Such happy splendor as itself,

Giving hints of joy.
Everything is subject to change,
To transform we must sacrifice

Ourselves, the way the tree surrenders
To autumn wind, wet and winter.

THE LIE

Many people
Travel in twos

Not from tenderness
And truth

More from fear
And convenience

GAME

We played a zero sum game.
From the end of the driveway

I saw her bumper sticker
"Love Wins."

As if love and win
Belong in the same breath

I inhaled.
She loves only with her mind.

OLD MAN AND THE FROG

An old man walks by a pond.

He sees a frog on a moss-covered log. As he passes, the frog speaks to him. The old man gently lifts and places the frog in his coat pocket.

After a few yards of walking, the frog leaps onto the lapel of the old man's worn topcoat. "If you kiss me, I will turn into a beautiful princess and grant you any wish."

The old man shakes the lapel of his coat and the frog falls back into the pocket. An hour later, the old man finishes his walk and sits on a log to rest.

The small green frog jumps from the pocket onto the log.

"I said, if you kiss me, I will grant you all of your dreams."

The old man stands and gently places the frog back into his coat pocket.

"I'm content to have a talking frog."

OLD MAN AND THE SEA

Coaching leaders is a lot like fishing.

At heart, I'm a deep-sea fisherman.

Marlin, tuna, mahi mahi . . .

I don't fish dolphin as they are our wiser ancestors. It just seems inappropriate to eat a wise ancestor.

Anyone who fishes whales, well, they ought to be shot—onsite, no trial, just a 9 mm to the head on the sandy shore.

I don't fish sharks. I leave those predators, sleek and formidable, to management consultants. They tend to like shark meat.

If I don't learn something from the fish I'm coaching in our first month, I reel in the line. All fishermen are learners; not all fish are.

My dad was a fisherman. He tried to teach me how to fish when I was a kid, "Fishing is waiting, son, waiting mostly. And making friends with silence." I was too impatient, but the seeds were planted.

I simply required a different kind of fish: leaders.

Corporations are a kind of aberrant school of fish. The kind of fish that kill the waters they swim in. Peter Drucker, a great fisherman, after many decades of seeing far off into the horizon wrote, "I believe that the 21st century will see the death of the corporation. It will be replaced by a hybrid organization, truly dedicated to people, planet, profit—serving society."

There are plenty of leaders claiming to be such fish. Especially, these new high-tech fish, called FAANG and the like. Make no mistake, they are barracuda with brains.

I wish Drucker were still fishing. He was a hell of a lot smarter fisherman than I'll ever be.

I am patient now. Catch one of these sleek, deep-water fish, and you can change the world. But first the fisherman has to learn how to fish the deep waters. And you cannot be afraid to lose the fish.

SMARTY PANTS

"All I want is for you
To accept me the way I am."

"Yes, and all I want is for you
To accept that I do not accept

You the way you aren't."

RARE

People do not choose,
They repeat

Patterns and projections,
The illusion of choice.

Forged in mind
Past and mind future.

Choice is simple and easy.

Natural like water
Trickling through a meadow
Or crashing down a mountain.

The way hawk meets thermals
And how children jump and smile
An infinity of impulse.

I trust such movement.

BRUCE LEE

The thing about the past is that it travels with you.

I left the concrete construction crews, then applied myself and did well when I returned to college in my mid-twenties. After, I found myself working for an airline—a plum job, running a team responsible for the international advertising in eighteen countries on four continents. While flying first class around the world, I would shake my head every once in a while, as only a few years back I was knee deep in wet cement. I spent five years fast tracking with the world's largest ad agency, and now I was client side, working for this international airline, a *corporate* guy.

I'm in a meeting with the Pacific region marketing managers and their boss. The boss—an Iranian man in his mid to late forties, snazzy dresser, everything just so—and I are arguing about something in the brand plan, and he calls me a liar. He tries to blame me for something he missed. Everybody knows, even one of his guys steps up for me, but he won't budge and says it again, "liar," glaring at me.

I've been a lot of things in my life, but a liar is not one of them. I lunge across the table, grab his silk tie, and snap down hard. The guy's jaw smacks the surface of the boardroom table. To his credit, Mr. Ahmadi pops up pretty quickly. Three of his managers have to hold him back. He's screaming in Iranian. Actually it's Persian—Farsi, I find out later—a lovely sounding language. "*Be Kiram. Bokhoresh!*" The others summon security, who escort the two of us out different entrances of the building.

My boss calls that night, asks if I'm okay, then tears a royal strip off. He says something about probation and orders me to see the Pacific Region Senior Vice President, Michael Chen, first thing in the morning.

"First thing ... tomorrow morning, Sean!" I hear the dial tone.

Michael Chen is a legend, the first Eurasian executive to ascend to the twenty-fifth floor, apparently a genius, and on the airline's executive committee. Mr. Chen is the Iranian guy's boss. I figure I'm toast, but I go to work anyways, take the spiral staircase between the twenty-fourth and twenty-fifth floor, and knock on Mr. Chen's partially open door.

He leaps from his chair and swings around the desk, fluid, like a leopard. Mr. Chen is much younger than I thought he'd be. He has the best features of both his parents, Swedish mother and Hong Kong Chinese father. I am about to speak.

"Tell me you did not grab Cyrus Ahmadi's tie yesterday and, in front of the Pacific region marketing team, smash his jaw into our twenty-second-floor boardroom table."

"I ..."

"Do you know anything about him? Anything!"

"I ..."

"Mr Ahmadi, who has worked for me for five years now, is the former *president* of Iranian Airlines, the world's largest airline, in the world's oldest culture. The night before the Shah of Iran fell, Mr. Ahmadi, his family, his wife, and four small children fled, on the last flight out of Iran at 3:00 a.m., with Revolutionary Guards firing bullets at the plane as it took off. They left with nothing, absolutely nothing. Do you even

understand what I am saying to you? They left with nothing."
He was shouting again.

I bow my head.

"Now Mr. Cyrus Ahmadi works as a manager in our airline,
headquartered here in Vancouver, where he has to put up with
the likes of you."

"He called me liar. I am not a ..."

Chen gestures for me to sit down. "I heard. You've got important
people that like you here, who see potential—brilliant, I think the
word is. And Cyrus has that damn, useless Iranian pride."

I'm thinking, "Hey, maybe I'm not fired yet." So I take a shot.

"Is it true, Mr. Chen, that you grew up in the streets of Hong
Kong with Bruce Lee, trained with him? Is it true you were his
best friend?

He nods.

I grin. "Well, I guess someone had to be his best friend."

"Get out of here," Chen says. "And I'd better not hear that
we need to send you to charm school. This is an airline; you're an
executive. You're not in a bloody boxing ring, Leclaire."

As I close the door behind me I look back. Chen is smiling
and shaking his head. He sent Cyrus Ahmadi and me on long
business trips together, until the inevitable happened. We grew
to like each other.

HUNGER

Emptiness
Is mental fasting.

A teacher
Declares,
"My mind would not dare
Have a thought
I did not want it to."

I drink
From his cup.
No longer thirsty
Mind
Empty.

THE TURN

The ending of a long-term relationship is a wide curve on a lonely highway.

The arc of the blacktop seems to keep going on and on and on. But I stay on the road, let go of the wheel; and I do not take detours. Diversions lead nowhere new, and I experience a loop the loop or two. That occurs. Nothing happens on God's amusement park by mistake.

But I feel what I must feel, and an amazing phenomenon occurs.

One morning, I'm driving in the car on I-95, and the air fills with sunlit silence.

I look in the rearview mirror, and there's nothing there except sky and space and ease. I am on a straight shot now, due north, bones aligned. I am humming some Top 40 song I used to hear on the radio when I was a kid, driven and guided by enthusiasm and the wondrous grace of the one song that we call the universe. Lessons have integrated, learning has happened, the engine is purring sweet. Forgiveness and mercy abound.

I am not so much a new man but rather the man I always have been.

I know, absolutely know, hands are no longer required on the wheel—the car drives itself. Spotify boots in. I hear Miles's first horn riff from "Kind of Blue," and my heart does not flinch. Feet in the present, eyes over the horizon.

Smiling.

BRIDGE

The cure for loneliness
Is solitude.

The bridge you cross
Is aloneness.

Being alone
Is not popular.
Popularity is overrated.

Spending time in solitude
Opens you to timeless wisdom.
Wisdom is in short supply.

Cross the bridge.

ENTRANCE

She asks, "Where is home to you?"
She expects, as most do, a common gesture—

Palms spread, arms open,
A half-twirl indicating

The lovely living room they stand in.
Instead, he smiles

Places his right hand on his heart.
She shows him the door.

His body crosses the threshold—
Alone,

But always home.

POTSHOT

My mind has worn me out today.

The mind possesses an ever-changing inner weather. The trick is not to interpret. Do not choose to have more thoughts about the already spinning thoughts.

We have that choice.

Discursive thinking is optional: Abort! Abort! Do *not* attach!

Thought storms can kill.

But we covet our thoughts, don't we?

They create accompanying images, impulses, feelings, body sensations—our stories—that weave what we call our identity. The mind is a meaning-making machine—this means that, that means this. But the mind can only make meaning, and meaning has nothing to do with Reality.

I learned how to write these short pieces from Paul Brunton. His books contain wisdom written in aphorisms—tiny jabs at the ego. Potshots.

All thought is dead.

Attaching to thought of any kind—pleasurable or painful—we deaden ourselves.

There are tons and tons and tons of fossils walking around this planet. I know, I know, not very compassionate of me.

Hey, it's just a friggin' thought!

7 NUGGETS

Not knowing is never the problem. Not wanting to know is.

Attachment bears bitter fruit.

Honor the part, serve the whole.

We do not learn by avoiding mistakes. We learn by making them.

If there is no way out, the best thing is to find a way further in.

It is hard to see through thoughts.

Clarity is medicine.

MEMORY

We live in a loft, a guy's place.

Third floor of an eighteenth-century house, more curves and angles than Beau's geometry set can measure. Low ceiling and steep stairs keep us attentive, or it's an instant lump on the noggin.

I'm making spaghetti dinner for Beau and his best buddy, Cameron.

They whoop it up in his room, planning something. The air changes when my son begins to plan something. "Dad where are those plastic boxes with all your writing stuff, those file things?"

"Why?" I yell from the kitchen.

"We need them!"

"In the basement behind the boiler, on the stacks."

Off they go, two crazed seven-year-old boys with a plan.

Thump, thump, thump. Five flights of wooden stairs, ten steps per flight, they descend the 60-degree pitches.

There's no Italian in my blood, but I make a mean spaghetti, with chicken chunks and pork hocks. I stir chopped farm stand tomatoes, garlic, onions, and kale, slowly. Keith Jarrett's *Koln Concert* elevates the room. Out the window I see two red-tailed hawks arc the cool evening air.

The thud makes the CD player jump. The floor shakes. "Geez-us! Beau, Bodhi!" Nothing. I walk down the first flight, open the door, still nothing, then giggling. Descend the next flight, turn.

Beau and his buddy have taken the Rubbermaid lids from the

folder boxes and are sliding down the stairs on the lids. Or they were. Now they're tangled on the second-floor landing like baby snakes coiled around each other in a ditch.

"We're surfers, Dad!"

WISDOM

In most people
Body and mind are not one.

Thought thinks
It knows but it knows not.

The body knows
It does not lie—body

Speaks its mind
Not with thoughts in the head

But with vibrations
Through the tissue

Pouring from the
Self

Listen
To that undivided

Being.

THE TRICKY PART

The atom of time
       Spins
     Splits
         Seconds are born
Sort of.
The skin of consciousness
Is matter
Or what we call
The universe
A song of light and awareness,
       That's the tricky part.
No one knows what light is;
       Matter is a different
Matter altogether.
Then love, love
       Unconditioned
     Conditioned by time,
Design flaws appear,
       But appearance is not Reality.
       Can you see the light of the universe
In everyone's eyes?

MYSTERY

When sex
Came to earth

Its twin death
Followed

Born of dust
Fire and mind

We are here
Even the sun

In all its hot
Glory cannot penetrate

The Mystery
What are we?

BOW

We are conduits for light.

Creative intelligence flows through us. All that moves through a quiet and clear mind is love.

I went to sit with an awareness teacher. I like her because she does not wear a robe, ascribes to no particular path or teacher or tradition, certainly no guru (how many of those terrific wolves in sheep's clothing have fallen?), and lives quietly in a hard-to-find log cabin in rural Vermont. A regular gal, yet not a regular gal, she probes, guides, asks disturbing questions. She's the electrician; I do the plumbing.

I sat with her for two hours or so. We talked, sipped green tea. We were quiet together. I have seen the vastness of the known universe in her eyes, and she has seen this in my eyes. Not much to say about that, just so utterly, astoundingly simple and lovely.

After the last visit, on the way home, my spine started to heat up—furious heat—then skull pain, like a migraine, but unrelenting, and so much more painful, such explosive pressure behind the eyes. *Wow.*

I've experienced these episodes—re-wiring—over the years but never with such intensity. It lasted three days. Then, the energy subsided and integrated. The electrical wiring inside of the body-mind transformed, the nerve bundles settled. Thoughts, discursive thinking, stopped for days. I could see clearly. It is hard to see through thoughts.

My mind kicked in again eventually, that's what minds do, and I remembered her suggestion.

"When in doubt, bow."

FREE AGENT

My son just left.

Five months into the coronavirus fiasco, he decided to go on a month-long road trip across America. "See what's up with people."

I've arranged a few hosted stops along the way in rural Georgia with a client, in Fort Worth with a friend, and in Santa Fe with my coach.

Beau is calmly excited; he's heard the stories of my time on the road: three years wandering overseas, then buying a blue van and rolling on the blacktop for 56,000 miles through the small towns of America. As my dad used to say, "When it comes to a real education, travel beats college hands down."

Now it is Beau's turn for the open road.

His favorite cousin, Joey, made him a playlist of 1,700 songs. As Beau pulls away from my apartment in New York, I have a vivid memory. His first day of kindergarten, I drop him off at the school building then sit in the car unable to move, drive away. Slowly, I pull the car under a willow tree by the rotary, sweet tears flow. I sit there with the engine running. And it occurs to me that I have a male mind but a female soul. My son is the same way.

And, now he's nineteen, a sophomore in college. Beau wants to see what is becoming of America. He does not follow popular political media or corporate-spun narratives; he likes to see things firsthand and make his own determinations.

"Do you think my car will make it to the Pacific Ocean, Dad?" He yells out the window.

Beau has a big view of things, "cycles," he says in our conversations, and he means millions of years. He thinks like a paleontologist.

His mother and I are somewhat concerned. But parents projecting their own fear onto their children can distort and even destroy a child's life. We gave simple guidance: When in doubt, common sense and caution prevail.

Nothing more, other than the old-school admonition, "Call your mother!"

Why do fathers say that? I want Beau to call *me* every night and tell me he is safe.

Beau is the very best of America. He doesn't drink, and he doesn't smoke or use drugs, a straight-A student; the man is courteous, polite, and he doesn't take life's twists and turns too seriously. And especially not himself. Beau is courageous and curious, a good friend to his crew of friends. A natural leader. Co-raising him is one of the best—*the* best—things I have done with my life. But he is in God's hands, always has been, not mine or his mother's. And that doesn't mean everything will go well on his journey or that he will safely return to us.

Pilgrimages are not about safety.

A HUMAN BEING

As an unwanted child I wanted,
Attention.

In my emboldened teens,
Fury.

Lost in my twenties,
Sex.

In my brooding thirties,
Respect.

Trudging the foothills of forty,
Mercy.

Mid-way up the mountain,
Gratitude.

In my sixties,
Peace
Without suspicion.

Stumbling toward seventy,
Joy.

BROADWAY

When Beau was four years old, I competed for a small but good part in a play on Broadway—small in the sense that as a talented but inexperienced actor, I could not get into too much trouble with the role, and good, because I was the first character onstage, the first to speak.

Actors wait a lifetime for such an opportunity; mine came in 90 days. I was in the right place at the right time with the right people. And I had a deliberate daily craft practice for twenty years. I was ready. I did a solid job at the initial audition with the casting director and got a call back, which I nailed. The role was in an unpublished Tennessee Williams play, *In Masks Outrageous and Austere*. Much to the bewilderment of my teacher and New York producer, Susan Batson, who orchestrated the opportunity, I did not go to the meeting with the director.

Artists must place their art first, but even Susan, who signs her letters and books, "Always in the Art," stayed home until her son was twelve. She didn't return to the stage until her son, Carl, (also in the business) told her to go back to work. Susan had to ease back on the mother role and jump fully into acting, producing, and teaching again.

It was as simple for me. If I got the job, my son would be in Boston, and I would be in New York and would not see him. I would not raise Beau. Raising a kid is being there—making lunches, making dinner, pulling splinters out of fingers, patching them up after bicycle spills, driving them to everything and everywhere, listening, endlessly listening. I would miss the nightly ritual of tubby, teddy, story in the big blue chair. I declined and went home to my son.

I never regretted the choice to wait for my time in theater.

This year, his mother and I spent three days touring and settling him into his dormitory for his first year of college in Washington, D.C. So, now I'm off to New York.

Ready to act.

7 EYES

Instinct
Guards
The gate
Of desire and
Fear

Intellect
Cuts
Like money
And an old
Razor

Impulse
Surfaces
Only in flesh
Blood and
Bone

Intuition
Flickers
In the mind
Like a lightning
Bug

Imagination
Soars
With wide wings
But
Cold feet

Intelligence
Draws
Its Wisdom
From holy
Water

Inspiration
Seeks
A vessel
For sacred
Fire

THE KISS

He just got tired of everything
The wandering, music blaring
Over town speakers, trains packed in
Like sardines, the smell, oh! the stink of people,
Seeking god and more good hash oil,
Yoga doga, the morning bells, Arati,
Champa sticks, sandalwood candles, smoke,
And the nightly chatter of lost seekers.
There was this leper—
There were many lepers.

A leper alone,
She begs in blue sari by the sea.
Beside the masala chai vendor,
At dawn the traveler stops excruciatingly close by.
A radical okayness suffuses his body.
Caught by the breeze of love,
He prostrates
Before the wretched old woman,
Kisses her rotting fingertips.
A dog barks.

THE FIELD

Barefoot in a muddy field
Wildflower and lemon trees

There is no space wide enough
To contain joy

Golden bees and wet toes
Vast goodwill standing

At the shore of a great silence
If you have not been rocked

By the Infinite
Then you are not alive

EGGS

After the fiasco at baby Jesus's creche on Christmas eve, I had the earnest desire to get things right the next holy days. I went with an idea for an exotic Easter egg hunt.

"Dad, why do you pray to Jesus, talk to Buddha, and dance with Shiva music?"

When you're a single parent and live alone with your kid, sometimes you just give the child your adult perspective. "Maybe I'm just confused, like a lot of people these days, Bodhi." I call him Bodhi when we have these religious inquiries. "But I think it has to do with globalization and the blending of cultures due to a dynamic increase in freedom of movement. There's a massive blending of things. Plus, Nietzsche might have been right. We do live in a deeply secular time. Basically, God is dead."

"God is not dead, Dad. He's sleeping." Beau tilts his head like a cocker spaniel, smiles, and grabs his mitt. "Let's play pitch." The week before, he had quietly employed his crayons to color a heart on the statue of Buddha seated by the telephone. A rainbow heart.

"Does Buddha celebrate Easter?" We finish tossing the baseball and sit in a few inches of snow.

"What do you think?"

"Hmmm. Everybody likes Easter eggs. Probably!"

We live beside a forest with a stream that moves fast during the spring. And when you're around fifty pounds and four feet high, that stream seems like a raging river.

On Easter morning I hide bunny eggs in the woods. In tree branch nooks, on mossy wet stones, in a wedge of thick blossoming buds, behind big rocks, on crystalline ice patches near the stream. I place a big chocolate bunny egg on a smooth stone jutting from the middle of the stream and a few smaller eggs under a lip of melting ice. Water swirls and splashes through the woods.

The notion that "God is sleeping," haunts me. More and more, though, I can hear God in the stillness of a forest, watching a sun set or rise, standing in a bed of sunflowers with their heads tilted toward the afternoon light, under the sound of wild geese flying low, in the joy I feel by a mountain creek.

I think a lot about Jesus at Easter. Our species hasn't learned much. If a Jesus or a Buddha or a Shiva appeared today in the flesh, we'd follow them for a while—praise and project our own holiness onto the poor guys—then kill them.

But this Easter morning is nothing but love and laughter and light. A father and a son on an egg hunt in the woods, climbing trees, slipping on ice, rolling in patches of wet snow, crouched low, reaching for the chocolate egg in the middle of the stream.

"In the waterfall, Daddy!"

A LIFE

I will die in New York on a sunny day, on a day I can almost remember.

I will die in New York on an easeful day—perhaps on a Sunday—as today is Sunday, in autumn. The park fills with people and sweet smiling children. One pig-tailed girl senses I am about to take my last breath, breathless. I will still know I am here, was here, stumbling among stumblers.

Into what? Wholeness?

This unity came long before this passing, delicious moment.

And another and another and … what do I remember?

Memory is a secretary—the files fling open. Bits of paper everywhere: a candle, the flame, fireflies in a field, a cat called Ram, willows, the Pacific Ocean, sheer granite, sunflowers, her lips, the swirl of sweet sex. They were close to love.

And a boy. I will remember a son, his kindness. I will remember my old friend time, how she dressed her moments with such perfect elegance.

A life.

Now breathless, seraphim descend, and a faint voice.

"Hey, mister, mister. Wake up, wake up!"

LOVE

(1)
Wind
Finds its voice
In the leaves
Leaves
Find their wings
In the wind

(2)
Kiss
Like juicy red
Raspberries
Coming
In the early morning
Heat

(3)
You
Burned us
At the stake
We return as
Fire

MARRIAGE

From I to other,
Maybe even
Thee, then
We.

JOY

No giving, no receiving,
Alchemy of love.

WITH GRATITUDE

I thank each of the reviewers who took the time to read *Stumbling into Joy* and offered words of encouragement. I am also grateful to Lloyd Resnick, my earnest and supportive first reader.

Much love to Marilyn Freedman, my editor, who helped shape the manuscript. She is a fierce and fun person to collaborate with. Thank you to wonderful book designers Alan Dino Hebel and Ian Koviak.

The poem TRANSFORMATION was inspired by eight-year-old Caden Salzano and was a joy to write. I am grateful to Wayne Muller for his contribution to the last poem in the book.

I deeply appreciate my leadership coaching clients, people who help make my life robust and rich through our soulful conversations.

I'm grateful to my youngest sister Pauline for the priceless laughter. And much love to my good friends; you know who you are. As Bobby likes to say, "They'll never take me alive!" All my closest friends are rebel angels.

Blessings to a long-time companion Kamala for the joys, challenges, and adventures during our time together.

I told my son that a writer gets to have two lives. The life you live and the life you write about. Both are challenging and sweet. Even the deepest heartbreak can be tender when a person is truly present. Joy is always there, waiting for us.

Thank you for reading *Stumbling into Joy*.

ABOUT THE AUTHOR

Sean is a poet, actor, and leadership coach. The founding partner of Sean Leclaire & Associates, he and his colleagues work with global business leaders. His first two books, *Hug an Angry Man and You Will See He is Crying*, and *Mud-Wrestling with my Mind*, are now followed by *Stumbling into Joy*, making a trilogy, of sorts. Sean's one-man play *Small Town Boys*, premiered at The Vancouver Fringe Festival in 2018, and his new play *LEELA* opens in London in 2022. He lives in a small town near Boston, and travels widely.